SCIENCE OF FUN STUFF

Pulling Back the Curtain on Magic!

by Sheila Sweeny Higginson
illustrated by Rob McClurkan

Ready-to-Read

Simon Spotlight
New York   London   Toronto   Sydney   New Delhi

SIMON SPOTLIGHT

An imprint of Simon & Schuster Children's Publishing Division
1230 Avenue of the Americas, New York, New York 10020
First Simon Spotlight edition June 2015
For information about special discounts for bulk purchases, please contact Simon & Schuster Special
Sales at 1-866-506-1949 or business@simonandschuster.com.
The Simon & Schuster Speakers Bureau can bring authors to your live event. For more information or to book an
event contact the Simon & Schuster Speakers Bureau at 1-866-248-3049 or visit our website at
www.simonspeakers.com.
Manufactured in the United States of America 0515 LAK
2 4 6 8 10 9 7 5 3 1
Library of Congress Cataloging-in-Publication Data
Higginson, Sheila Sweeny, 1966– author.
Pulling back the curtain on magic / by Sheila Sweeny Higginson. — First edition.
pages cm. — (Science of fun stuff)
Audience: Ages 6–8
ISBN 978-1-4814-3701-1 (pbk.) — ISBN 978-1-4814-3702-8 (hc) — ISBN 978-1-4814-3703-5 (eBook) 1. Magic
tricks—Juvenile literature. 2. Magicians—Juvenile literature. I. Title. II. Series: Science of fun stuff.
GV1548.H48 2015
793.8—dc23
2015010821

CONTENTS

CHAPTER 1
Pay Attention!

Your eyes are focused on the man in the black suit. He waves a silk scarf in the air and then stuffs it into his hat. Then he taps the hat three times with his magic wand. Alakazam! The scarf disappears, and a snow-white dove flies out of the hat.

The crowd oohs and aahs. It looks like magic, but it's time to stop and take a closer look. In the pages of this book, you'll find out what's really going on. It's not magic at all— it's science!

Magicians have been thrilling people with their tricks since the time of the ancient Greeks and Romans, and probably even before that. "How can a trick be science?" you might wonder. It's not as if the magician mixed up a batch of chemicals that instantly turned the scarf into a dove.

An illusion is something that looks different from what it really is, and magic is all about illusion. The magician's scarf only appeared to transform into a living creature. Science explains why the audience believes the trick. Scientists are just starting to study magic seriously. Now you can study the science of magic too.

The art—and science—of magic relates to distraction and misdirection. It's a balancing act. If you want to be a successful magician, you have to use distracting actions, such as waving your right hand and telling your audience to watch your right hand very closely. These large actions keep your audience from noticing smaller actions, such as how you were secretly dropping a coin into your pocket with your left hand at the same time. To understand why that works, you need to know about the human brain.

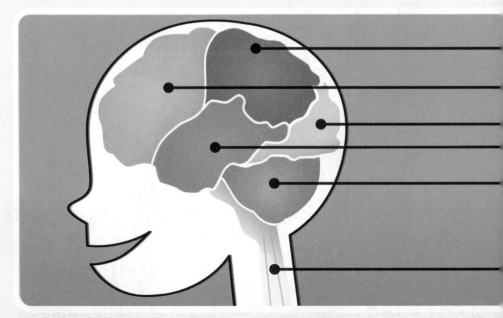

The human brain is an amazing organ. The largest part of the brain is the cerebrum. It controls all the things you do voluntarily, such as pushing the X button on your video game remote when you want to start a new game. The cerebrum also contains all your memory, and it gives you the power to think. The parietal, frontal, occipital, and temporal lobes are all part of the cerebrum. Your brain has other parts too, such as the cerebellum, which controls movement and coordination. And there's also your brain stem, which is in charge of all the actions that keep your body alive—such as breathing air and digesting food.

— parietal lobe (language and touch)

— frontal lobe (judgment and memory)

occipital lobe (sight)
— temporal lobe (hearing, comprehending sounds and pitches)

— cerebellum (balance and coordination)

— brain stem (breathing, heart rate, temperature, and many other important functions)

Your brain works so well because it is made up of about 85 billion neurons. Neurons are microscopic cells—cells so small they are visible only through a microscope. The neurons transmit information to and from different parts of your body. Neurons are found throughout your nervous system, which is made up of your brain, your spinal cord, and all the nerves that branch out through your body. These neurons have been working hard since before you were even born!

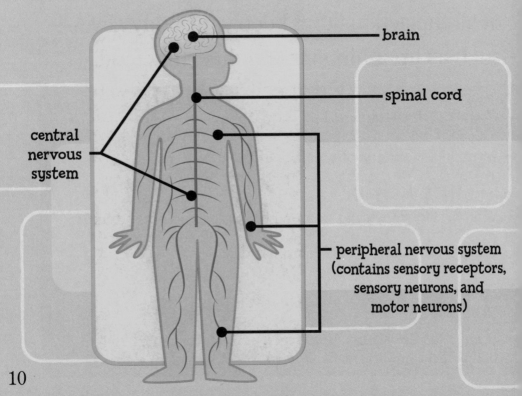

brain

spinal cord

central nervous system

peripheral nervous system (contains sensory receptors, sensory neurons, and motor neurons)

As you've grown, your body has been creating connections between the neurons. These connections help the information flow freely.

The more you do things over and over, the smoother the pathways in your brain become. Things you do every day—such as brushing your teeth—become so automatic, you don't even have to think about them anymore.

Magicians have, in a way, been studying the human brain for thousands of years. They know that when your brain is used to doing things a certain way, it's a lot easier to trick it! For example, if you hear a loud noise, you automatically turn to look in that direction. Magicians can use this information to "hide" something while you are distracted and looking the other way. Scientists have learned from magicians too. They now know that when the brain focuses its attention on one thing, it ignores what's happening on the sidelines.

Your brain is amazing, but it's not perfect. You may think you know everything that's going on around you, but your brain isn't really able to focus its attention on more than one thing at once. Magicians know that, and they also know that sudden and unusual changes in your environment will grab your focus.

Magicians know a lot about how a person's attention span works. Do you? Imagine that you're watching your favorite television show when a loud crack of thunder booms. And then there's a flash of lightning. What happened to your attention? Do you think your eyes would still be focused on the TV, or would you look outside the window when you saw the lightning? Would you hear what the actors said when the thunder boomed?

Your attention works like a reflex. It's distracted by sudden, unusual changes in the environment. It steers your perception, the same way a camera focuses on one image and can zoom in on that image but doesn't see anything outside the frame. A good magician knows just how to lead someone's attention so the person sees only what the magician wants them to see!

CHAPTER 2
The Principles of Magic

Misdirection

This is the most basic tool that every successful magician needs in his toolbox. Misdirection leads the audience's attention away from a secret move.

For example, a magician holds a ball up and tells the audience to look at it. While holding the ball up, the magician might slip another ball into his or her own pocket. No one in the audience notices that happening. Why?

There are special neurons in your brain called *mirror neurons*. When you watch a person doing something, mirror neurons help you see what that person is feeling while they are performing that action. And these mirror neurons lead to people having joint attention, which is when people all pay attention to the same thing.

The Palm

In this basic trick the magician secretly holds an object in a hand that you think is empty. Magicians practice squeezing small items, such as coins, very tightly in their palms. Then the magician quickly puts his hand out, facedown, so that it looks completely open, but it really isn't. Your brain is so used to thinking that there can't be anything in an open hand that you believe there's nothing there, without seeing for sure that there isn't something there.

The Switch

A magician secretly exchanges two objects. In one classic card trick, a magician asks a volunteer to pick a card. Then the

magician switches another card he had already chosen with the one the volunteer selected, so it appears that the magician is reading the volunteer's mind. To do this trick, the magician has to practice moving the cards without a lot of motion, and misdirecting his volunteer's attention while doing the trick.

The Ditch

A magician secretly gets rid of an object, such as

dropping a coin into your pocket. Again, the magician needs to practice the movements of the trick so that the drop is effortless, while using misdirection to make you focus on something else.

The Steal and Load

The magician secretly grabs and moves an object. An object, such as a scarf, is hidden somewhere out of the audience's view—for example, in the magician's pocket. Using a bit of misdirection, the magician reaches into his pocket and quietly "steals" the scarf, then "loads" it into his hand to make it seem as though it magically appeared.

HOWARD
the Great

Scientists have also learned that when we see something out of the ordinary, it sticks in our memories. Think about it. If your classmate came to school in her pajamas, a year later you'd probably remember exactly what she'd worn. You probably wouldn't remember what any of your other classmates wore on that day, though.

Our brains also prefer things that are funny. In fact, we like humor so much that it distracts us from unfunny things that happen at the same time. A magician might use fake fish in his act and say, "Pick a cod,"—instead of "Pick a card." He knows that if he can get the audience to laugh, it will be the perfect time to make a secret move.

23

CHAPTER 3
A Sense of Wonder

So now we know magicians like to trick our brains. But the brain isn't the only body part magicians use to trick people. The brain is also connected to the sensory system. This system includes all the parts of your body that help you see, hear, taste, touch, and smell. When a magician touches your shoulder during a trick, the neurons in your skin send a message up to your brain that says, "Did you feel that? Sensory information coming in!" You probably won't even notice that he lightly stuffed a scarf into your pocket at the same time.

The sensory system processes information in precise ways. One magician believed that an audience would follow a coin in his hand more closely if he moved it along a curve instead of a straight line. Scientists discovered that the magician was right. People's eyes tend to follow a curved motion from beginning to end smoothly, while our eyes jump from the start to the finish of a straight line.

Some tricks work because the human body tends to get used to its environment. That's why your eyes need a minute to reset after you've been outside in the bright light.

Your muscles also get used to how they're being used. A magician can use this science to his advantage.

In one simple trick a person is told to stand with their arms down at their sides. The magician pushes against the person's arms and asks her to try to lift them. When the magician lets go, the person's arms will magically float up by themselves! That's because the muscles want to keep doing what they've been doing. So the person's brain is telling her arms to keep pushing upward.

Magicians such as Harry Houdini put their own bodies to work. Houdini was a great escapist. He trained his body for incredible feats of magic. He could hold his breath for more than three minutes. He could twist and turn his body to escape from ropes, chains, and straitjackets.

The bones, joints, and muscles of your musculoskeletal system help you stand, walk, and catch a ball. Joints are the places where two or more bones meet. Skeletal muscles are attached to the bones. Some people are hypermobile, or double-jointed. That means that they are able to move their joints beyond the normal range. Many people believe hypermobility was one of the keys to Houdini's success. He could bend his arms and shoulders in ways that most people can't.

Don't worry. You don't have to be double-jointed to be a great magician! You don't even need much muscle power at all to perform most magic tricks. Take the "apple through the straw" trick. The magician holds a straw in one hand. He shoves it straight through an apple. It seems as though the magician used incredible strength to pierce a hard apple with a flimsy plastic straw.

The magician's real power is science! The secret to the trick is the way the magician holds the straw—with his thumb on the end, sealing it tightly. Air is trapped inside, which makes the straw stiff and able to pierce the apple like an arrow.

If you try this trick at home, be careful not to hit your hands with the straw, or you might be hurt.

CHAPTER 4
The Grand Illusion

Here's another popular trick.

The secret to this trick is that the magician uses two spoons, one spoon to show the audience, and another that he will secretly bend. As the magician gives the first unbent spoon to the audience to examine, he uses misdirection—such as a joke—to hide that he's bending a second spoon. When the audience gives him the first spoon back, he will secretly switch it with the one he has bent.

He will then hold the bent spoon in the middle and start to wiggle it back and forth. He will stare at the spoon, pretending to use his mind to bend it. When he stops shaking it, he shows his audience that it's bent!

We have to go back to brain science to see why the spoon trick works.

Remember the neurons you have in your brain? They're in your eyes, too. Some vision neurons respond to the corners of an object. Others respond to the edges. Different neurons sense motion differently too. They get mixed up when the spoon is shaken, and they send a signal to the brain that makes it think that the spoon is straight.

Magicians can also use tools such as mirrors to trick the eyes. Thomas Tobin invented a special illusion trick in 1865. It's called the Cabinet of Proteus, and it revolutionized magic.

Someone enters the cabinet and closes the door. When the door is opened again, it looks like they've vanished. They haven't—but the mirrors inside the cabinet make it look like as though they did.

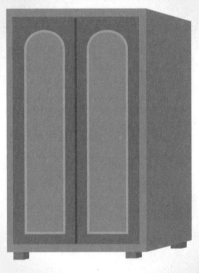

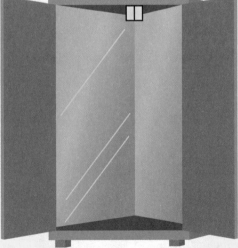

Other magicians use more complicated tools to create illusions. French magician Jean Eugène Robert-Houdin loved playing with new technology. He used electromagnets to create his "Light and Heavy Chest" trick back in the 1800s.

A metal plate was hidden at the bottom of the chest. The magician would call a child onstage to demonstrate how easy it was to lift the box. After the child put the chest back down on the floor, the magician secretly flipped a switch that turned on an electromagnet hidden under the floor. The magnet would attract the metal plate in the chest so strongly that the chest couldn't be picked up.

Then Robert Houdin would ask a muscular adult man to try to lift the box. With his magical powers of switch-flipping, the magician had now turned a very light box into one that was impossible to lift! The audience thought it was magic, but it was really science and technology!

Science
OF FUN STUFF
Expert
— ON —
Magic

Congratulations! You've learned the secrets behind some magic tricks—and the *science* behind them.

Throughout history, magicians have vowed to never share the secrets behind their tricks. Scientists, of course, are all about figuring out the secrets. So now it's time for you to decide. Are you a true magician, or a true scientist?

Hey, kids! Now that you're an expert on the science of magic, turn the page to learn even more about magic, history, geography, and how to perform a simple card trick!

Harry Houdini:
The World's Most Famous Magician

Say the word "magician" to almost anybody, and the first name mentioned will most likely be Harry Houdini. He is considered the most famous magician who ever lived.

Houdini was born in 1874 in Budapest, Hungary, and was given the name Erik Weisz. When he began performing magic, Erik took the stage name Harry Houdini as a tribute to the French magician, Jean Eugène Robert-Houdin.

Fame did not come easily to Houdini. For the first few years of his career, he performed mostly card tricks and simple escapes. He made enough money to get by, but as a magician his act wasn't special enough to get him noticed.

But by the late 1890s he came up with an idea that made him stand out from the crowd. He called it the "Challenge Act." In this act Houdini bragged that he could escape from any handcuffs brought to the theater by a member of the audience.

My brain is the key that sets me free.
— Houdini

Fans loved bringing handcuffs to Houdini's shows and watching him wriggle out of them. Soon magic lovers everywhere were talking about the Great Houdini!

Houdini then made his Challenge Act even harder. Houdini said he could not only escape from any handcuffs, but he could also escape from any place in the world.

Houdini escaped from inside locked crates thrown into rivers. He escaped from jail cells, and he even survived leaping from bridges while handcuffed. Audiences were dazzled. They had never seen anyone like Harry Houdini.

Houdini died on, of all days, Halloween in 1926.

Seventy-six years after his death, the US Postal Service honored Houdini with a special postage stamp. What makes it special? The stamp does a trick! In normal light the stamp just looks like a picture of a young Harry Houdini. But when you look at the stamp through a special viewer, Harry appears to be shackled in chains!

A Card Trick for You

WHAT YOU NEED:

A regular deck of playing cards

WHAT YOU DO:

1. If you are performing this card trick in front of more than one person, ask for a volunteer to shuffle the cards. If you're doing this trick for one friend or family member, have that person shuffle the cards. Let the person take as long as they want to shuffle.

2. When the deck is handed back to you, spread all the cards facedown on a table. Tell your volunteer to "pick a card, any card" and not show it to you.

3. If there are other people, have your volunteer show the card to the other audience members. If you're showing this trick to one person, have them stare at the card, and tell them to concentrate on it.

4. You are using misdirection—because as the person is concentrating on the card or showing it to other people, you will put all the others back into a pile. Then cut the pile in half and quickly sneak a peek at the bottom card in your left-hand pile. Practice this at home so you can do it as quickly as possible.

5. Ask your volunteer to place their card facedown on the top of the pile in your right hand.

6. Place the left-hand pile on top of the right-hand pile. Tell your volunteer (or audience), "I will now find your card." Say a few "magic words" (such as "abracadabra") to make it even more dramatic.

7. Now spread the cards face up on the table, putting the pile down on the left and then spreading the cards to the right. Look for the card that was at the bottom of your left-hand pile. JUST TO THE RIGHT will be the card your volunteer selected!

Famous Magicians Around the World!

Everyone in the world loves magic! This list of famous magicians includes magic acts from all over the globe.

Jean Eugène Robert-Houdin (1805-1871)

Jean Eugène Robert-Houdin, born in Blois, France, was Harry Houdini's idol. Robert-Houdin never planned on becoming a magician—he actually wanted to be a clock maker! However, when his clock-making textbooks were delivered, a mistake had been made. Instead of the books he'd ordered, he had been sent two books on magic! Robert-Houdin read them and fell in love with magic. Today he is known as the father of modern magic.

Dante the Magician (1883-1955)

Born in Copenhagen, Denmark, Dante traveled all over the world, performing his magic in vaudeville (live entertainment shows in the early twentieth century), films, the theater, and even on television. Dante was known for his elaborate stage illusions. He also became famous for saying "Sim Sala Bim!" (a nonsensical phrase taken from a children's song) during his performance to acknowledge applause.

Harry Blackstone Sr. (1885-1965)

Harry Blackstone was born in Chicago, Illinois, and is credited with creating one of the most popular magician's tricks—sawing a person in half. In this trick a magician cuts through a wooden box, seemingly cutting the person inside in half. The person then rises out of the box unharmed. Known as the "Great Blackstone," his career started in vaudeville in 1904, but Blackstone later made a name for himself by performing for American troops during World War II.

Siegfried and Roy (Siegfried Fischbacher, born 1939, Roy Horn, born 1944)

Siegfried Fischbacher and Roy Horn were born in Germany. Roy met Siegfried in 1957 while working on an ocean liner. Siegfried was a steward who entertained guests with magic tricks on the side. Roy became Siegfried's assistant, and together they created a magic act using exotic animals. Audiences were used to seeing rabbits disappear, but Siegfried  and Roy could make a cheetah disappear! From 1990 to 2003 Siegfried and Roy had one of the most popular shows in Las Vegas.

David Copperfield (born 1956)

Born in Metuchen, New Jersey, David became the youngest to gain admission into the Society of American Magicians when he was twelve years old! By the time David was sixteen, he was already teaching a class in magic at New York University. Copperfield is known for his stunning illusions, such as making the Statue of Liberty "disappear" and walking *through* the Great Wall of China. David has received twenty-one Emmy Awards plus the Living Legend award from the United States Library of Congress.

Being an expert on something means you can get an awesome score on a quiz on that subject! Take this

SCIENCE OF MAGIC QUIZ

to see how much you've learned.

1. An illusion is?

a. a type of scarf

b. a rabbit

c. something that looks different from what it really is

2. When you push a button to start a new video game with your friends, what part of your brain are you using?

a. the cerebrum

b. the frontal lobe

c. the brain stem

3. Neurons are

a. bones

b. muscles

c. microscopic cells

4. If a magician tells you to look at a card while he's hiding a scarf, he is using

a. misdirection

b. humor

c. mathematics

5. What was an effect of Houdini's training his body?

a. he was small

b. he could hold his breath longer than the average person

c. he was incredibly fast

6. Our brains prefer things that are

a. sad

b. funny

c. romantic

7. A magician secretly puts a playing card in your pocket. In magic, this is known as

a. the ditch

b. a prank

c. the palm

8. When everyone looks at something a magician is holding up at the very same time, this is an example of

a. the magician's voice

b. the magician's eyes

c. joint attention

Answers: 1. c 2. a 3. c 4. a 5. b 6. b 7. a 8. c